FANTASTIC
FACTS
ABOUT
HIGH-TECH
FARMS
WARREN SINGER
REDBACK
publishing

First Published 2026 by
Redback Publishing
Suite 6, 13a Narabang Way,
Belrose NSW 2085
Australia

www.redbackpublishing.com
info@redbackpublishing.com

ISBN 978-1-761402-16-6

Author: Warren Singer
Editor: Simone Saba
Designer: Redback Publishing

Originated by Redback Publishing

Acknowledgements
Abbreviations: l—left, r—right, b—bottom, t—top, c—centre, m—middle
We would like to thank the following for permission to reproduce photographs: (Images © shutterstock)
p25b - Paul R. Jones / Shutterstock.com, p28tl - Larry Cumpton / Shutterstock.com, p28mr - Sheryl Watson / Shutterstock.com, p28b - Steve Lovegrove / Shutterstock.com, p29b - anatra_76 / Shutterstock.com, p30tl - Serge Goujon / Shutterstock.com, p30tml - Djohan Shahrin / Shutterstock.com

A catalogue record for this book is available from the National Library of Australia

CONTENTS

High-Tech Farms

With over eight billion people in the world, farms need to use high-tech methods to produce enough food to feed us all. Whether the farm is on land, or a fish farm in the sea, farmed animals and crops are all part of a complex interaction between technology and nature.

SUBSISTENCE FARMING

Small communities don't need large farms. They can survive when everyone has a vegetable garden, a few chickens, and a cow in the home paddock to produce food. This type of 'subsistence farming' is becoming less and less common across our planet.

LEAVING THE FARM

All around the world, people are moving from rural areas to cities, where they cannot grow enough food to feed themselves.

CITIES NEED FOOD

Massive farms need to use technology to help grow the quantity of food that is needed to feed all the people living in cities.

FUTURE FARMS

Farms of the future will have so much technology running them that they will not look like today's farms at all.

BIGGER CITIES

In the next few decades, 70% of the world's population will live in cities. All of them will need food that they have not grown themselves.

WATER

Climate change is affecting the availability of water for farming, so water supply will be one of the main problems that future farmers will need to deal with.

Harvesters

The world's biggest wheat farms cover over 10,000 hectares (approx. 25,000 acres). That's bigger than some small countries. High-tech harvesters are a necessity to keep these huge farms operating.

HOW BIG?

Some harvesting machines are 5 metres (16 feet) high, and 11 metres (36 feet) long. That's about the size of a double-decker bus.

COMBINE HARVESTERS

A combine harvester makes work much easier for the farmer. It cuts the wheat stalks from the fields and separates the seeds from their dry, outer covering, called the chaff.

HEADERS

A corn head and a wheat grain cannot be gathered in the same way by a combine harvester. Different attachments are required depending on the crop, these are called headers.

BIGGEST FARMS

The biggest wheat farms in the world are in China and India. For these farmers, high-tech harvesters are a necessity.

BREAD

It takes one square metre (10 square feet) of wheat plants to make a loaf of bread. Think about all the people in the world who eat bread every day. That equates to an enormous quantity of wheat that has to be grown in fields.

Irrigators

Farmers cannot rely on rain to ensure their crops grow. They need expensive irrigation systems that supply water whenever and wherever it is needed.

AVOIDING WASTE

Farmers rely on technology to irrigate as efficiently as possible. These watering methods include micro-irrigation which delivers small amounts of water to each plant through specific methods like drip irrigation. Drip irrigation delivers water directly to plant roots, drop by drop.

TYPES OF IRRIGATORS

MOTORISED IRRIGATORS - some farmers use motorised irrigators, which move by themselves across a field. A moving irrigator can be over a kilometre long.

PIVOT IRRIGATORS - pivot irrigators do not move along a field. Instead, they spray water around in a circle. The arms on this machine can be hundreds of metres long.

20% OF THE WORLD'S CROPS

About a fifth of all the crops in the world are watered using artificial irrigation.

WATER SOURCE

The irrigator can pump its water from a channel that the farmer has to dig beside the fields. Farmers pump the water they need from underground, or they divert it from a nearby river.

COMPUTERS

Using computer programs and AI, farmers can ensure that crops are only watered at times when the effect will be maximised.

Sensors that detect sunlight, air and soil moisture, and many other factors, all feed into computer programs that decide when and where water is delivered to crops.

High-Tech Animal Care

To livestock farmers, their animals are their source of income. Livestock that receives the best care will produce high returns for the farmer.

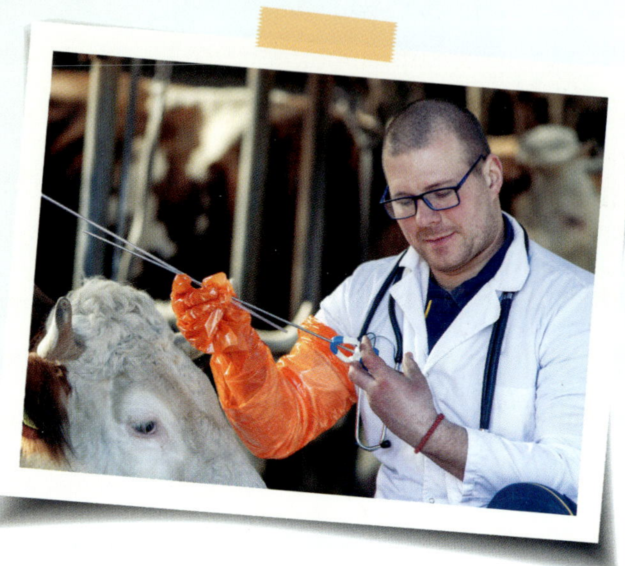

ARTIFICIAL BREEDING

Cattle that have less fat in their meat, or cows that produce the best milk, can all be bred using artificial methods. In this way, a whole herd of young animals with the best possible qualities can be produced in a short time, without having to wait decades for that to happen naturally.

MONITORING EVERY ANIMAL

Farmers can now monitor the health and condition of every animal in a herd. After placing electronic sensors on the animals, farmers use a computer screen back at the farmhouse to find out where every animal they own is located on the farm, and what is happening to them.

DISEASES

A disease that could destroy a whole herd can be picked up quickly using the electronic sensors on animals. Early intervention could help avoid a health disaster.

FEEDING AUTOMATICALLY

With so many supplements and additives that need to be added to animal feed, there are now even more demands on the farmer's time than in the past. Automatic feeding systems can lighten this workload and improve livestock health at the same time.

SELF-DRIVE HERDING

The technology for self-driving herding vehicles is under investigation. The positive and negative effects on livestock are yet to be known for certain, but avoiding any harm to valuable animals is a priority.

High-Tech Tractors

Tractors are now high cost, high-tech vehicles, with air-conditioned cabins, computer screens, internet connectivity and comfortable interiors.

SOLAR-POWERED

Solar panels on tractors can ensure that all the electronic equipment inside the vehicle keeps going throughout the whole day while the farmer is working.

AUTOMATIC STEERING

Tractors are vehicles with multiple functions on a farm. They still do the traditional tasks of hauling, ploughing and cutting. Additional work for the farm tractor now includes using automatic, self-guided steering so that very accurate and straight rows can be ploughed.

GPS

Tractors use GPS to work out exactly where they are in a field. This enables them to automatically ensure that every part of the field is ploughed to the same standard, without any damage to the land.

CAMERAS

Full-view cameras in tractors show what is happening all around the vehicle as it works. The live feed could be sent to the farmhouse office, as well as being viewed inside the cabin.

CONNECTED TRACTORS

Every tractor on a farm can be digitally connected with all the other vehicles on the farm, or even with neighbours. This makes exchanging vital information quick and easy, and it improves work safety in the fields.

Drones on Farms

Drones on farms can do more than help a farmer find lost animals.

PASTURES

The view from the camera on a drone can show a farmer the condition of the pasture in every corner of the farmland. Without even going out and doing a personal inspection, a farmer can decide if cattle need to be moved to a different paddock where there is more grass.

FERAL PREDATORS

Feral predators can be monitored by cameras on a drone, warning a farmer that action is needed.

CROP SPRAYING

Drones can be used to spray crops with pesticides or fertilisers. They allow the spray to be placed in precise locations, reducing the overspray that occurs if large spraying equipment is used.

SCARECROWS

Drones could be the scarecrows of the future, chasing off birds that damage crops.

WEATHER

The use of drones on farms depends on having fine weather. Strong winds and rain will mean that a drone cannot be used.

SEEDING

Drones equipped with special attachments can disperse seeds across a large area very quickly. This is called aerial seeding.

Electric Power to Every Field

Solar power now allows farmers to use electronic devices in every remote corner of the property.

SOLAR POWER

Solar panels installed throughout the farm can power electric fences, and water pumps to pump water to dams and troughs.

BATTERIES

Solar power will only work when the sun is shining. Battery storage will extend the use of power from sunlight so that it can be used at night or on overcast days as well.

SOLAR IRRIGATION

Automatic irrigation equipment can be powered using solar panels. This means that expensive cables do not have to be installed to connect the equipment to an electric power supply.

FARM SECURITY

Thieves will target hidden areas of a property where they can enter and steal livestock without being detected. A solar-powered security system can be used at every boundary to protect the farm.

SENSORS

Computer sensors throughout the farm need power to work and transmit their data back to the farmhouse. Solar power can do this from every location where the farmer needs to keep an eye on conditions.

Precision Agriculture

Knowing how to use computer programs created for farm management is now a necessity for any modern farmer.

Precision agriculture is now considered the most efficient way that farmers can manage their farms. It involves using technology to monitor every aspect of the crop cycle and of keeping livestock.

Precision agriculture encourages the best use of natural and financial resources, improving the farm as a business and making it more profitable.

COMPUTERS AND SOFTWARE

Computer programs help the farmer by using all the data collected by sensors and drones across the farm. The aim is to make the use of water, pesticides, stock feed and fertilisers very precise. This results in less waste and less pollution.

LOWERING COST AND POLLUTION

Keeping the use of pesticides and fertilisers to a minimum, based on the actual need as shown by sensors, means the cost is lower. There is also less pollution of surrounding areas.

SENSORS

Farmers no longer need to waste water on a whole field, when sensors can tell them the precise spots where water and fertiliser are needed.

High-Tech Dairy

The milking of hundreds of cows in a dairy herd used to be done by hand, twice a day. This exhausting work can now be done by robot milking machines.

ROBOT MILKING

Cows learn to come to the milking shed twice a day, and they line up to be milked by the automatic milking machinery. Robot milking machines do not need a farmer to be there when the cows are being milked. The machines do the whole process.

CLEAN AND TEST

Milking machines do much more than collect the milk. Some machines are so automated they can clean the cow and themselves, attach themselves to the cow, and do preliminary tests on the milk as it is produced.

BULK TANK

Milk flows to a holding vat where it is kept cold. A milk tanker comes to the farm regularly, collects all the milk and takes it to a dairy factory. The milk from many farms is tested and pasteurised at the factory before machines pour it into bottles and cartons.

MILK PRODUCTS

Cheese, yogurt, cream, ice-cream and butter all come from milk. In factories, these foods are made with large machines.

THE BIGGEST

The biggest milking machines can milk thousands of cows at once. Some milking sheds are bigger than a football field.

Vertical Farming

We need farms for our food, but they take up a lot of flat space. Is vertical farming the way of the future?

GOING VERTICAL

Instead of growing vegetables out in flat fields, vertical farmers plant them in stacks or walls that are placed next to each other. Some farms use horizontal structures on top of each other, but these need artificial lighting at the lower layers.

Vertical farming relies mainly on a nutrient-enriched water supply, rather than on soil to grow the plants.

Careful control of the water, temperature, sunlight and humidity make it a high-tech operation.

Some vertical systems claim they can produce as much or even more product as traditional farming land.

NOT FOR LIVESTOCK

Vertical farming is only viable for fruit and vegetable farming. Livestock and grain farms still need a lot of open space to grow.

High-Tech Packing

Farm produce has to be packed and transported in perfect condition. This is harder than you might think!

BAGGING

Automatic bagging machines add the right weight of produce to bags and seal them. Without machinery to do this work, the produce would take longer to get to shop shelves and would spoil more often.

EGGS

Packing thousands of eggs every day is not an easy task. The damage rate can be high when done by hand. Packing machines can do the work quickly and with less damage, meaning that the eggs can be sent off to shops and remain fresher on the shelves for longer.

ADDING GAS

Various sorts of gases are added to packages to keep meat, vegetables and fruit fresh for longer. Adding carbon dioxide to fruit and vegetables slows down their activity and stops them from rotting quickly.

GRAINS

Machines sort, clean and bag grains to turn them into products that an average consumer can buy and handle. It would be almost impossible to do this work by hand, considering the large amounts of grain that are produced.

COTTON GIN

Cotton farmers need access to a cotton gin, which separates the seed from the white, fluffy fibres. The clean cotton is then pressed into bales. The name, cotton gin, is a combination of the two words, cotton and engine.

High-Tech Silos

SILOS

When farmers harvest large amounts of grain, such as wheat or corn, they cannot send it straight to a factory to be made into food. They first store the grain in massive silos, which look like tall cylinders.

SAFETY

The silos keep the grain safe from the weather, and from mice and insects. That is why silos are mostly made from metal or concrete, with no gaps where vermin can get into them.

BIGGEST SILOS

Some of the biggest silos in the world are over 40 metres (131 feet) high and wide. That's as high as a 13-storey building. Ensuring the stability of a full cylinder that high is an impressive engineering achievement.

DIGITAL MONITORING

The silos have machinery to move the grain in and out, and from one spot to another. The temperature and humidity in modern silos are monitored by computers. This is necessary since grain in silos can explode into a fire if not stored properly.

Getting Around the Farm

When a farm is as big as a small country, farmers need special ways to get around.

SUGAR TRAINS

TANKERS

HELICOPTERS

UTES

ATVS

SMALL AIRPLANES

TRACTORS

HORSE RIDING

MOTOR BIKES

Moving Livestock

ROAD TRAINS

Livestock are valuable living things. Farmers need ways to transport their stock that keeps them safe, healthy and ready for market.

DROVING

HORSE FLOATS

RAILWAY

LIVESTOCK SHIPS

AIRPLANES

TRUCKS

Glossary

bale	large bundle
chaff	dry, outer covering of grains
combine harvester	harvesting machine that cuts grain and separates it from the chaff
divert	change the flow
droving	moving livestock by walking them overland
fertiliser	chemical added to make plants grow
intervention	action to stop or change something that is happening
pasteurise	heat to kill germs
pesticide	poison to kill pests
preliminary	at the beginning
subsistence farming	only growing enough for one's own needs
trough	long tub to hold water or animal feed
viable	able to work well or survive

Index